SAGES OF THE SUBCONTINENT

BIOGRAPHIES OF INDIA'S GREATEST SPIRITUAL MASTERS

DR. JAGADEESH PILLAI

|| "Dedicated to all who seek to understand and appreciate Indian culture and tradition." ||

Contents

Contents

Prayer

"Om Bhadram Karnebhih Shrunuyaama
DevaahBhadram Pashyemaakshabhiryajatraah
SthirairangaistushtuvaamsastanoobhihVyashema
Devahitam YadaayuhSwasti Na Indro
VridhashravaahSwasti Nah Pooshaa
VishwavedaahSwasti Nastaarkshyo ArishtanemihSwasti
No Brihaspatir DadhaatuOm Shantih, Shantih, Shantih"

The literal meaning of this mantra is: OM. O Gods! Let us hear auspicious words from our ears. O reverent Gods! Let us behold propitious visions from our eyes, let our organs and body be stable, healthy, and strong. Let us do that which is pleasing to the gods in the life span allotted to us. May Indra, inscribed in the scriptures, bring us fortune! May Pushan, the knower of the world, grant us prosperity! May Trakshya, who vanquishes enemies, bestow us with blessings! May Brihaspati bring us success!
OM Peace, Peace, Peace.

About The Author

Dr. Jagadeesh Pillai is a renowned Guinness World Record holder, writer, and researcher hailing from Varanasi, also known as the abode of Lord Shiva. With a Ph.D. in Vedic Science and a range of creative ideas and achievements, he is a true polymath. He is the author of more than 100 books including Research Publications. Although his roots can be traced back to Kerala, the people of Varanasi hold him in high regard and affectionately consider him one of their own.

Dr. Pillai has achieved four Guinness World Records in the following subjects:

"Script to Screen" - In this record, Dr. Pillai produced and directed an animation film within the shortest time possible, breaking the previous record set by Canadians. He has also received numerous national and international awards and recognitions for this achievement.

Longest Line of Postcards - For this record, Dr. Pillai created a line of 16,300 postcards on the occasion of the 163rd anniversary of Indian Postal Day. The event also included a questionnaire about the Indian flag.

Largest Poster Awareness Campaign - Dr. Pillai designed an awareness campaign on the subject of "Beti Bachao - Beti Padhao" (Save the Girl Child - Educate the Girl Child) to achieve this record.

Largest Envelope - In tribute to the Indian Prime Minister's

"Make in India" initiative, Dr. Pillai created a 4000 square meter envelope using waste paper to achieve this record.

Attempted - **70000 Candles on a 210 kg Cake** - To celebrate the 70th Indian Independence Day, Dr. Pillai attempted to light 70,000 candles on a 210 kg cake, which was recorded in World Records India.

Attempted - **Documentary on Dhamek Stupa of Sarnath in 17 Languages** - Dr. Pillai attempted to create a documentary on the Dhamek Stupa of Sarnath, dubbing it in 17 different languages. The result of this attempt is currently awaiting confirmation from the Guinness World Records.

Dr. Pillai is skilled in teaching the Bhagavad Gita, a Hindu scripture, and is popular among young people. He has helped many young people improve their lives through his motivational teachings.

In addition to teaching, he has composed and sung numerous Sanskrit Bhajans and patriotic songs.

He has also written and directed several short films and documentaries for awareness campaigns, and has volunteered with the police in both UP and Kerala to spread awareness about various issues through videos and photography.

Incredibly, he has produced and directed over 100 documentaries about the city of Varanasi, all on his own.

He has also helped and guided more than 25 boys and girls to achieve world records through creative and innovative methods. He is a multifaceted person who uses his intellect and the blessings given to him by God to excel in various areas. He is both a teacher and a student, always learning and teaching, and is able to master any subject he comes across.

He is a selfless social activist and motivational speaker who has overcome struggles and failures to become a successful and enthusiastic individual with a rich life experience.

In addition to his work with the Bhagavad Gita, he is also an efficient Tarot card reader, Astro-Vastu consultant, and a talented singer and composer. He has sung the entire Ram Charita Manas and Bhagavad Gita in his own compositions, and has sung the phrase "Lokah Samastha Sukhino Bhavantu" in 50 different languages. He is currently working on a detailed and scientific study of Vedas, Upanishads, Puranas, and the Bhagavad Gita. He has also composed and sung the Hanuman Chalisa and Gayatri Mantra in 108 and 1008 different compositions, respectively.

Awards - Four Times Guinness World Records, Winner of Mahatma Gandhi Vishwa Shanti Puraskar, Mahatma Gandhi Global Peace Ambassador, Kashi Ratna Award, Dr. APJ Abdul Kalam Motivational Person of the Year 2017, Mother Teresa Award, Indira Gandhi Priyadarshini Award, Bharat Vikas Ratna Award, Udyog Ratna Award, Vigyan Prasar Award, Poorvanchal Ratn Samman.

ॐॐॐ

Preface

"Sages of the Subcontinent: Biographies of India's Greatest Spiritual Masters" is a collection of biographical accounts of some of the most revered spiritual leaders of India. These figures have not only left an indelible mark on the spiritual landscape of the subcontinent, but have also influenced the lives of countless individuals across the world. From Adi Shankara, the 8th century philosopher and theologian, to Mahatma Gandhi, the father of the Indian nation, each of these sages has made a unique contribution to the spiritual and cultural heritage of India. Through their teachings, writings, and actions, they have inspired generations to seek a deeper understanding of the human condition and the nature of the divine. This book aims to provide an introduction to the lives and legacies of these remarkable individuals, and to explore the enduring relevance of their wisdom for contemporary readers.

In this book, you will learn about the life, teachings and contributions of Adi Shankara, Kabir, Ramakrishna Paramahamsa, Mahatma Gandhi, Ramana Maharshi, Swami Vivekananda, Jhanesvar, Ramprasad Sen, Lahiri Mahasaya, Guru Nanak, Sant Ravidas and Tulsidas, who have been selected as some of the greatest spiritual masters of India. Each of these figures has left an undeniable mark on the spiritual and cultural heritage of India and the world. They have influenced the lives of millions of people through their teachings, writings and actions. Their wisdom has been passed down through generations and still holds relevance in the contemporary world.

In this book, we delve into the personal lives of these sages and explore the context in which they lived and how that influenced their teachings. We examine the key aspects of their teachings, the practices they advocated and the impact they had on their followers. The book also explores the influence of these spiritual masters on the broader society and culture of India, and how their teachings continue to shape the spiritual landscape of the subcontinent.

The book is intended for readers who are interested in gaining a deeper understanding of the spiritual traditions of India and the lives of the sages who have shaped them. Whether you are a student of spirituality, a seeker of wisdom, or simply someone who is fascinated by the rich spiritual heritage of India, this book offers a unique and engaging introduction to some of the most revered spiritual leaders of the subcontinent.

ᐡᐡᐡ

ONE
The Sage of Sages: Adi Shankara

Adi Shankara, also known as Shankara Bhagavadpada, was one of the most influential philosophers and spiritual leaders of ancient India. He is best known for his philosophical teachings on Advaita Vedanta, a non-dualistic interpretation of the Vedas, which has had a profound impact on the spiritual and philosophical traditions of India and continues to be studied and revered to this day.

Shankara was born in 788 CE in the state of Kerala, in South India. He is said to have been a prodigy, mastering the Vedas and other religious texts at a young age. He is also said to have been a realized soul, with many stories of his spiritual powers and enlightenment experiences.

At the age of eight, Shankara was initiated into sannyasa,

the monastic life, by his guru, Govinda Bhagavatpada. He then began his travels, visiting holy places and engaging in philosophical debates with scholars and other spiritual leaders. He is said to have defeated many of these scholars in debate, establishing the superiority of his Advaita Vedanta philosophy.

Shankara's Advaita Vedanta philosophy teaches that the ultimate reality is the non-dual Brahman, and that the individual self (Atman) is identical to Brahman. He taught that the ultimate goal of spiritual life is to realize this non-dual reality and to merge the individual self into the universal self. He also emphasized the importance of devotion to God, or Ishvara, as a means of attaining this realization.

Shankara's teachings have had a significant impact on the spiritual and philosophical traditions of India. His commentaries on the Upanishads and the Bhagavad Gita are still widely read and studied today. He also established mathas, monasteries, across India to spread his teachings and to provide a place for spiritual practice and study.

Shankara's influence can also be seen in the Bhakti movement, which emphasizes devotion to God as a means of spiritual realization. Many of the great saints and poets of the Bhakti movement, such as Ramanuja and Madhva, were deeply influenced by Shankara's teachings.

Yes, Adi Shankara was one of the greatest sages of ancient India. His teachings on Advaita Vedanta continue to be studied and revered today, and his influence can be seen in many spiritual and philosophical traditions of India. His emphasis on devotion to God and the ultimate goal of realizing the non-dual Brahman have provided a great source of inspiration for many spiritual seekers over the centuries.

❦❦❦

"The ultimate goal of human life is self-realization." - Adi Shankara

TWO

THE POET SAINT: THE LIFE AND LEGACY OF KABIR

Kabir was a 15th century Indian mystic poet and saint, known for his teachings of devotional mysticism and his unique blend of Hindu and Muslim beliefs. Born in Varanasi, India, Kabir lived a simple life as a weaver, but his poetry and teachings attracted a large following of devotees from both Hindu and Muslim communities.

Kabir's poetry is renowned for its deep spiritual insight and its ability to convey complex spiritual concepts in simple, everyday language. He emphasized the importance of a personal relationship with God and the power of devotion in attaining spiritual realization. He also spoke out against the caste system and religious hypocrisy, which earned him the wrath of both Hindu and Muslim religious leaders.

One of the most significant aspects of Kabir's teachings is

his emphasis on the unity of God, and the idea that all religions lead to the same ultimate realization. He taught that the true path to God is not through rituals or external practices, but through the inner experience of devotion and love. Kabir's teachings are reflected in his poetry which is spiritual and devotional in nature, and often uses imagery and metaphor to convey his message.

Kabir's legacy has been passed down through the Kabir Panth, a tradition of followers who have kept his teachings alive through the centuries. His poetry continues to be widely read and studied in India, and his message of unity, love, and devotion has resonated with people of all religious backgrounds.

Kabir was really a unique and influential figure in the Indian spiritual tradition, who through his poetry and teachings, emphasized the importance of personal devotion to God, and the unity of all religions. His legacy continues to inspire spiritual seekers to this day.

ᐅᐅᐅ

"The true sign of intelligence is not knowledge but imagination." - Albert Einstein, influenced by Indian spirituality.

THREE
THE SAINT OF MIRACLES: RAMAKRISHNA PARAMAHAMSA

Ramakrishna Paramahamsa, also known as Sri Ramakrishna, was a 19th century Indian saint and mystic, who is considered one of the most important spiritual figures of modern India. He is known for his teachings on the unity of all religions, and his emphasis on the importance of direct personal experience of God through spiritual practices.

Ramakrishna was born in 1836 in a small village in West Bengal, India. From a young age, he showed an intense spiritual inclination and had many profound spiritual experiences. He practiced a wide range of spiritual disciplines, including devotion to the Hindu goddess Kali, and the Muslim practice of Sufism, and had realizations in each one of them. He is said to have had many miraculous experiences, and is considered by many to be a fully realized soul.

Ramakrishna's teachings emphasize the unity of all religions and the idea that all paths lead to the same ultimate goal of realizing God. He taught that the true goal of spiritual life is to experience God directly, through practices such as devotion and meditation, rather than simply acquiring knowledge about God. He also emphasized the importance of service to others as a means of spiritual advancement.

Ramakrishna's teachings had a profound impact on many of his followers, including his most famous disciple, Swami Vivekananda, who went on to become one of the most influential spiritual leaders of modern India. Ramakrishna's teachings also had a significant impact on the spiritual and cultural revival of India in the late 19th and early 20th centuries.

Surely, Ramakrishna Paramahamsa was one of the greatest spiritual figures of modern India. His teachings on the unity of all religions and the importance of direct personal experience of God continue to inspire spiritual seekers to this day. His emphasis on service to others and the importance of spiritual practices has also had a lasting impact on the spiritual traditions of India.

ᐅᐅᐅ

"The highest truth is truth of non-dualism." - Ramana Maharshi

FOUR

THE PROPHET OF NONVIOLENCE: MAHATMA GANDHI

Mahatma Gandhi, also known as "The Father of the Nation" in India, was a political and spiritual leader who is best known for his philosophy of nonviolent resistance and his role in the Indian independence movement. He is widely considered one of the most influential figures of the 20th century, and his message of nonviolence continues to inspire people around the world.

Gandhi was born in 1869 in British-ruled India, and was educated in England. After returning to India, he struggled to establish himself as a lawyer but eventually decided to leave the profession and devote himself to the struggle for Indian independence. He began to develop his philosophy of nonviolence and civil disobedience, which he believed was the only way to achieve Indian independence without resorting to violence.

Gandhi's philosophy of nonviolence was rooted in the principles of truth and love. He believed that nonviolence was the highest form of resistance and that it was the only way to achieve lasting change. He also believed that nonviolence was not just a political strategy but a way of life, and that it should be practiced in all aspects of one's life, including personal relationships and interactions with others.

Gandhi's message of nonviolence and civil disobedience was instrumental in the Indian independence movement. His campaigns of non-cooperation and non-violent resistance against the British government, including the famous Salt March, led to the withdrawal of British rule in India in 1947.

Gandhi's message of nonviolence and his philosophy of Satyagraha (truth force) has had a profound impact on world history and continues to inspire civil rights and freedom movements all over the world. His teachings have influenced many leaders and activists such as Martin Luther King Jr and Nelson Mandela.

Mahatma Gandhi was a political and spiritual leader who is best known for his philosophy of nonviolence and his role in the Indian independence movement. His message of nonviolence and civil disobedience continues to inspire people around the world to this day, and his legacy continues to be a source of inspiration for those who struggle for freedom and justice.

❦❦❦

*"Be the change you wish to see in the world." -
Mahatma Gandhi*

FIVE

THE MASTER OF ADVAITA: RAMANA MAHARSHI

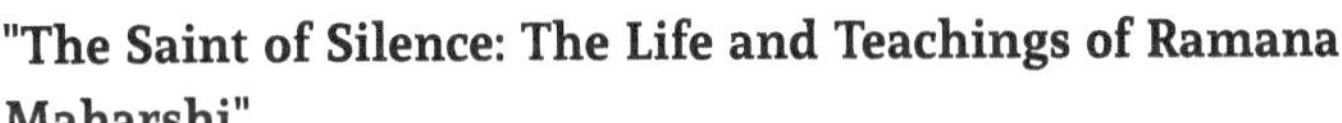

"The Saint of Silence: The Life and Teachings of Ramana Maharshi"

Ramana Maharshi, also known as Bhagwan Sri Ramana Maharshi, was a 20th century Indian sage and jivanmukta (liberated soul), who is considered one of the most important teachers of Advaita Vedanta, a non-dualistic interpretation of the Vedas. His teachings emphasized self-enquiry as the path to self-realization and liberation.

Ramana Maharshi was born in 1879 in Tamil Nadu, India. From a young age, he had an intense interest in spiritual matters and had an experience of enlightenment at the age of 16, which marked the beginning of his spiritual journey.

After this experience, he left home and spent several years in deep meditation and self-enquiry, eventually settling at the holy hill of Arunachala, where he began to attract a large number of devotees.

Ramana Maharshi's teachings are based on Advaita Vedanta, the philosophy that the ultimate reality is the non-dual Brahman and that the individual self (Atman) is identical to Brahman. He taught that the ultimate goal of spiritual life is to realize this non-dual reality and that the path to this realization is self-enquiry, which involves examining the nature of one's own self to discover the ultimate reality. He also emphasized the importance of devotion and surrender to God, or Ishvara, as a means of attaining self-realization.

Ramana Maharshi's teachings have had a significant impact on the spiritual traditions of India and continue to be studied and revered to this day. His emphasis on self-enquiry as the path to self-realization has been particularly influential, and his teachings have been a source of inspiration for many spiritual seekers.

No doubt, Ramana Maharshi was a great sage and jivanmukta, who through his teachings on Advaita Vedanta, emphasized the path of self-enquiry as the means to attain self-realization and liberation. His teachings continue to inspire spiritual seekers to this day, and his legacy continues to be a source of inspiration for those who seek the ultimate truth.

ॐॐॐ

"The one who sees the Lord within all beings, and all beings within the Lord, does not see duality." - Ramakrishna Paramahamsa

SIX

THE SAINT OF SOUTH INDIA: SWAMI VIVEKANANDA

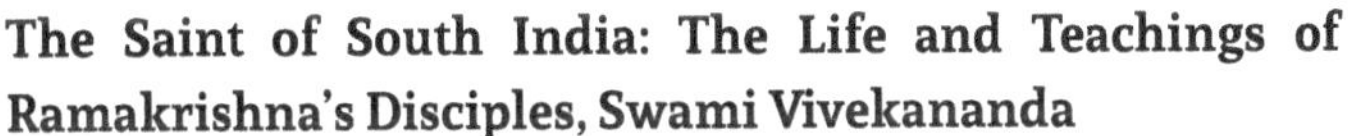

The Saint of South India: The Life and Teachings of Ramakrishna's Disciples, Swami Vivekananda

Swami Vivekananda, born Narendranath Dutta, was a 19th century Indian monk, and one of the most prominent disciples of Ramakrishna Paramahamsa. He is considered one of the most influential spiritual leaders of modern India, and his teachings on Vedanta and the unity of all religions continue to inspire spiritual seekers to this day.

Vivekananda was born in 1863 in Calcutta, India, and had a strong inclination towards spirituality from a young age. He met Ramakrishna at the age of 20 and was deeply influenced by his teachings. After Ramakrishna's passing,

Vivekananda renounced the world and took sannyasa (the monastic life) and became known as Swami Vivekananda.

Swami Vivekananda's teachings are based on the Advaita Vedanta philosophy, the same as his guru, Ramakrishna. He emphasized the unity of all religions, and the idea that all paths lead to the same ultimate realization. He taught that the true goal of spiritual life is to experience God directly, through practices such as devotion and meditation, rather than simply acquiring knowledge about God. He also emphasized the importance of service to others as a means of spiritual advancement.

Vivekananda's message of unity and tolerance resonated with people around the world, and he became one of the most prominent spiritual leaders of his time. He traveled extensively, giving lectures and speeches on spiritual matters, and was invited to speak at the World's Parliament of Religions in Chicago in 1893, where he made a lasting impression on the audience and was referred to as "the most remarkable man present".

Swami Vivekananda's teachings have had a significant impact on the spiritual traditions of India and continue to be studied and revered to this day. His emphasis on the unity of all religions and the importance of spiritual practices has also had a lasting impact on the spiritual traditions of India.

Swami Vivekananda was one of the most prominent disciples of Ramakrishna Paramahamsa and a great spiritual leader of modern India. His teachings on Advaita Vedanta and the unity of all religions continue to inspire spiritual seekers to this day. His emphasis on service to others and the importance of spiritual practices has also had a lasting impact on the spiritual traditions of India.

ৡৡৡ

"All the world is full of suffering. It is also full of overcoming it." - Helen Keller, influenced by Indian spirituality.

SEVEN

THE SAINT OF MAHARASHTRA: JÑĀNEŚVAR

The Saint of Maharashtra: The Life and Teachings of Jñāneśvar

Jñāneśvar, also known as Jñāneśvar Bhaṭṭa, was a 13th century Indian saint and poet, who is considered one of the most important spiritual figures in the Bhakti movement in Maharashtra, India. He is best known for his spiritual poetry, particularly the Jñāneśvari, which is considered one of the greatest works of Marathi literature and an important source of spiritual teachings.

Jñāneśvar was born in 1275 in the present-day state of Maharashtra, India. He was a child prodigy and displayed spiritual inclinations from a young age. He was initiated into sannyasa, the monastic life, by his guru, Gahininath. He then spent most of his life traveling, teaching, and spreading devotion to God through his poetry and spiritual teachings.

Jñāneśvar's teachings are based on the Bhakti tradition, which emphasizes devotion to God as the path to spiritual realization. He taught that the ultimate goal of spiritual life is to realize God, or Ishvara, through love and devotion. He also emphasized the importance of selfless service to others as a means of attaining spiritual realization.

Jñāneśvar's poetry, particularly the Jñāneśvari, is renowned for its spiritual insight and ability to convey complex spiritual concepts in simple, everyday language. It is considered one of the greatest works of Marathi literature and an important source of spiritual teachings.

Jñāneśvar's teachings and poetry have had a significant impact on the Bhakti movement in Maharashtra and continue to be studied and revered to this day. His emphasis on devotion to God and selfless service has also had a lasting impact on the spiritual traditions of India.

Jñāneśvar was a great saint and poet of Maharashtra, India, who through his teachings and poetry emphasized the importance of devotion to God and selfless service as the path to spiritual realization. His legacy continues to be a source of inspiration for spiritual seekers in Maharashtra and beyond.

ॐॐॐ

"The mind is the source of all bondage and
liberation." - Jhanesvar

EIGHT

THE POET-SAINT OF BENGAL: RAMPRASAD SEN

The Poet-Saint of Bengal: The Life and Teachings of Ramprasad Sen

Ramprasad Sen, also known as Ramprasad "Ramprasad Sen" or simply Ramprasad, was a 18th-century Indian poet-saint from Bengal, known for his devotional poetry and his devotion to the Hindu goddess Kali. His poems, which are written in Bengali and Braj Bhasha, are considered some of the most important examples of Bengali literature and continue to be widely read and celebrated to this day.

Ramprasad was born in 1718 in a small village in Bengal, India. He was a devotee of the goddess Kali from a young age, and began composing devotional poetry in her honor. He worked as a clerk in a wealthy landowner's estate, but spent much of his free time singing and composing devotional songs. He later left his job to become a wandering minstrel, traveling across Bengal and singing his poems in the temples of Kali.

Ramprasad's poetry is renowned for its deep spiritual insight and its ability to convey complex spiritual concepts in simple, everyday language. He emphasized the importance of devotion to Kali as the path to spiritual realization, and his poems often express his longing for union with the goddess. He also emphasized the importance of selfless service to others as a means of attaining spiritual realization.

Ramprasad's poetry and teachings have had a significant impact on the Bhakti movement in Bengal, and his devotional songs are still widely sung and performed in temples and devotional gatherings in Bengal. His emphasis on devotion to Kali and selfless service has also had a lasting impact on the spiritual traditions of India.

Ramprasad Sen was a great poet-saint of Bengal, India, who through his poetry and teachings emphasized the importance of devotion to Kali and selfless service as the path to spiritual realization. His legacy continues to be a source of inspiration for spiritual seekers in Bengal and beyond. His devotional poetry is considered one of the most important examples of Bengali literature and continue to be celebrated to this day.

ৡৡৡ

"You are not a drop in the ocean. You are the entire ocean in a drop." - Rumi

NINE

THE SAINT OF THE HIMALAYAS: LAHIRI MAHASAYA"

The Saint of the Himalayas: The Life and Teachings of Lahiri Mahasaya

Lahiri Mahasaya, also known as Babaji, was a 19th century Indian saint and yogi, who is considered one of the most important spiritual figures in the Kriya Yoga tradition. He is said to have attained a state of spiritual realization, and to have passed on the knowledge and techniques of Kriya Yoga to many of his disciples.

Lahiri Mahasaya was born in 1828 in a small village in Bengal, India. From a young age, he showed a deep interest in spiritual matters and began practicing yoga and meditation. He eventually attained a state of spiritual realization and began teaching others the techniques of Kriya Yoga, which he considered to be the most direct and effective means of attaining spiritual enlightenment.

Kriya Yoga is a spiritual practice that involves a set of techniques for controlling the breath and directing the energy of the body towards spiritual realization. Lahiri Mahasaya taught that the ultimate goal of spiritual life is to realize the true self, or Atman, and that Kriya Yoga is the most direct and effective means of attaining this realization. He also emphasized the importance of devotion to God, or Ishvara, as a means of attaining spiritual realization.

Lahiri Mahasaya's teachings have had a significant impact on the Kriya Yoga tradition, and his disciples have continued to teach and pass on the knowledge and techniques of Kriya Yoga to this day. His emphasis on the importance of spiritual practices such as yoga and meditation as the path to spiritual realization continues to inspire spiritual seekers to this day.

Surely, Lahiri Mahasaya was a great saint and yogi of the Himalayas, who through his teachings on Kriya Yoga and the importance of devotion to God as the path to spiritual realization. His legacy continues to be a source of inspiration for spiritual seekers in the Kriya Yoga tradition and beyond.

ᐁᐁᐁ

"The goal of human life is to be one with the divine." - Guru Nanak

TEN

THE SAINT OF THE NORTH: SIKH GURU, GURU NANAK

The Saint of the North: The Life and Teachings of Sikh Guru, Guru Nanak

Guru Nanak, the founder and first guru of Sikhism, was a 15th century Indian saint and spiritual teacher who is considered one of the most important figures in the history of the Indian subcontinent. He is known for his teachings on the unity of God, the equality of all human beings, and the importance of selfless service to others.

Guru Nanak was born in 1469 in the present-day state of Punjab, India. From a young age, he displayed an inclination towards spiritual matters and began to question the religious practices of his time. He eventually renounced the world and traveled extensively, spreading his message of the unity of God, the equality of all human beings, and the importance of selfless service to others.

Guru Nanak's teachings emphasize the importance of devotion to one God, the importance of living a truthful and honest life, and the rejection of the caste system. He also emphasized the importance of earning a living through honest means and sharing one's wealth with others. He taught that the ultimate goal of spiritual life is to realize the presence of God in all things and to merge with God.

Guru Nanak's teachings have had a significant impact on the Sikh tradition and continue to be studied and revered to this day. His emphasis on the unity of God, the equality of all human beings, and the importance of selfless service has also had a lasting impact on the spiritual traditions of India.

Guru Nanak, the founder and first guru of Sikhism, was a great saint and spiritual teacher of the Indian subcontinent, who through his teachings emphasized the importance of devotion to one God, the equality of all human beings, and the importance of selfless service to others. His legacy continues to be a source of inspiration for spiritual seekers in the Sikh tradition and beyond.

ꖂꖂꖂ

"We are not human beings having a spiritual experience. We are spiritual beings having a human experience." - Teilhard de Chardin

ELEVEN

THE SAINT OF THE PEOPLE: RAVIDAS

Sant Ravidas, or Raidas, was a saint, a mystic poet and a great spiritual figure in India who lived in the fifteenth and sixteenth centuries. He is one of the most beloved figures in the Indian spiritual pantheon and is revered in Hinduism, Sikhism, Buddhism and Jainism. Sant Ravidas was a social reformer who inspired and led the underprivileged people of his time to work for a better and more fulfilling life for all.

Sant Ravidas was born into a family of leather tanners in a small village in modern-day Varanasi, India. His family belonged to the untouchable caste, and despite the discrimination they faced, Sant Ravidas chose to focus on the inner light within himself and to live in harmony with all people. He dedicated his life to devotion, kindness, and service to God and humanity.

Sant Ravidas taught a simple, practical and spiritually-minded message of universal acceptance and compassion. He believed that ultimate truth and salvation could be found through devotion to God and selfless action, and he created the idea of the "Guru -Chela" relationship, in which all should serve one another, the Guru being the teacher and the Chela being the learner.

Ravidas's teachings were widely accepted and embraced by many followers from all castes, making him a great influence in Indian social and spiritual life. His widespread influence was also felt beyond the region, with people from all over the country turning to his guidance. He founded several ashrams (spiritual centers) throughout India and his teachings achieved great popularity among the common people of the country.

Sant Ravidas had a great impact on Indian society by using the power of his teachings to promote equality and justice for those of lower castes and those who were discriminated against. His selfless dedication to the cause of social justice was instrumental in bringing dignity and respect to those oppressed by Hindu society.

His teachings have continued to be an inspiration to people of all classes and backgrounds. His teachings have been collected and published in a set of holy texts called "Shabad Granth" and "Guru Granth Sahib", which have been widely read and studied in India and abroad.

Overall, the life and teachings of Sant Ravidas are a source of great strength and hope, particularly for those who still suffer injustice and discrimination in the modern world. His legacy lives on in the hearts and minds of those who follow his teachings and strive to bring equality and justice to the world.

ᐯᐯᐯ

"The true sign of intelligence is not knowledge
but imagination." - Albert Einstein

TWELVE

LIFE AND TEACHING OF TULSIDAS

Goswami Tulsidas (also known as Tulsidasji) was a celebrated poet-saint in India known for his great literary and poetic works that reverberate with spiritual horizons. He is known for creating the widely popular and widely read Ramcharitmanas (The Sacred Lake of the Acts of Rama), an epic monumental work that is considered to be his main legacy. It is widely popular in not only India but also other countries like Bangladesh and Fiji, where it is widely read and recited during Hindu festivals.

Born in Uttar Pradesh in the 16th century, Tulsidasji was deeply spiritual from an early age, making a pilgrimage to the island of Jammu & Kashmir in his youth. He resided in the ashram of Jagatguru Ramanand, who is believed to have initiated him into the Vairagi tradition and imbued him with the values of devotion and self-realization.

An avid traveler and a prolific writer, Tulsidas dedicated much of his life to the cause of Hindu Dharma and served as a spiritual teacher to many of his admirers and admirers of his works. He regarded Lord Rama as the embodiment of divine love and compassion and wrote extensively on the subject. His works include poetry in the Awadhi language, commentary on texts of the Bhagavad Gita, the Ramayan, the Mahabharat and other ancient scriptures. His most famous work, the Ramcharitmanas (The Sacred Lake of the Acts of Rama) is an important masterpiece of the Hindu tradition and is widely considered to be Tulsidas' magnum opus.

In it, Tulsidas Ji retells the entire story of the Ramayan from a humanistic, rather than a divine point of view, and redefines the path of bhakti (devotion) for a modern audience. By extolling the virtues of Lord Rama's exemplary life and by describing His love for his people, Tulsidas seeks to inspire people of all backgrounds to strive for the good and to build a society based on justice, truth, and righteous behavior.

The moral and humanitarian principles espoused by Tulsidas is not only inspiring, but also noteworthy. His works have had a great influence on not only Hinduism, but also Indian culture. He is held in high regard throughout India and his Ramanand sect is considered one of the four main sects of Hinduism.

Goswami Tulsidas is an admirable figure in the Hindu tradition and his influence is still felt in India today. His powerful teachings and inspiring works will continue to be influential works of literature and will continue to serve as a source of wisdom and inspiration for generations to come.

ᐳᐳᐳ

"India is the cradle of the human race, the
birthplace of human speech, the mother of
history, the grandmother of legend, and the
great grandmother of tradition." - Mark Twain

Other Books Of The Author

1. The Moments When I Met God
2. Kashiyile Theertha Pathangal
3. GURU GYAN VANI
4. Abhiprerak Gita
5. ASSI SE JAIN GHAT TAK
6. Hopelessness of Arjuna
7. The Soul and It's True Nature
8. Sense of Action (Karma)
9. Action through Wisdom
10. Action through Wisdom
11. THEORY AND PRACTICAL OF EVERY ACTION
12. LOGICAL UNDERSTANDING OF THE SUPREME
13. THE IMPERISHABLE SUPREME
14. Yatra Nishadraj se Hanuman Ghat Tak
15. Yatra Karnatak Ghat se Raja Ghat Tak
16. Yatra Pandey Ghat se Prayagraj Ghat Tak
17. Yatra Ranjendra Prasad Ghat se Dattatreya Ghat Tak
18. YaatraSindhiya Ghat se Gwaliar Ghat Tak
19. Yatra Mangala Gauri Ghat se Hanuman Gadhi Ghat Tak
20. Yatra Gaay Ghat Se Nishad Ghat Tak
21. MAA GANGA, GHATEN EVM UTSAV
22. Ganga Arti Dev Deepavali evam Any Utsav
23. Potentials of Digitalized India
24. VEDIC CONSCIOUSNESS
25. A Brief Introduction to Vedic Science
26. Kashi ke Barah Jyotirling
27. IMPACT OF MOTIVATION
28. Let's have a Milky Way Journey
29. Color Therapy in a Nutshell

30. Rigveda in a Nutshell
31. Yajurveda in a Nutshell
32. Samveda in a Nutshell
33. Atharva Veda in a Nutshell
34. Ayushman Bhava - Ayurveda
35. Srimad Bhagavad Gita and Upanishad Connection
36. Srimad Bhagavad Gita - an attempt to summarize each chapter.
37. Facts and Impact of Nakshatra
38. Astro Gems - NAVARATNA
39. Ekadashi - A Concise Overview
40. A Concise View of Hanuman Chalisa
41. Inspirational Gita
42. Nakshatraranyam
43. Summary of 18 Mahapuranas
44. Synopsis of 18 Upa Puranas
45. Rigvediya Upanishads
46. Shukla Yajurvediya Upanishads
47. Krishna Yajurvediya Upanishads
48. Samavediya Upanishads
49. Atharvavediya Upanishads
50. The Seven Great Sages
51. From Rocket Scientist to President Dr. APJ Abdul Kalam
52. The Visionary's Voice - Quotes of Dr. APJ Abdul Kalam
53. The Wisdom of Swami Vivekananda: Insights and Inspiration from a Legendary Spiritual Teacher
54. Ayurvedic Remedies from the Garden
55. Sages and Seers
56. Rising Strong – Motivational Stories of Women
57. Beyond Flames -Mystery stories of Funeral Ghat Manikarnika
58. The Origins of Tulsi: A Look at the Mythological Roots of the Plant"

59. The Holistic Cow: A Look at the Physical, Spiritual, and Cultural Importance of Cows in India
60. Arts of Healing
61. Exploring the Divine
62. Understanding Five Elements
63. The Etymology of Ram
64. Symbols of India
65. Voice of Change (About Speeches of Great Men)
66. She Speaks (About Speeches of Great Women)
67. Patriotism on Celluloid – Brief About Patriotic Films
68. The Music of Motivation: A Brief Guide to Inspirational Film Songs
69. Unlocking the Secrets of the Dashopanishads
70. A Cultural Mosaic
71. Ancient Traditions, Modern Minds
72. Beneath the Surface
73. From Temples to Ashrams

ৡৡৡ

Contact

DR. JAGADEESH PILLAI

PhD in Vedic Science

Four Times Guinness World Record Holder

Winner of Mahatma Gandhi Vishwa Shanti Puraskar and Global Peace Ambassador

Gemology, Astro & Vastu Consultant - Spiritual Counselor

Consultant for designing World Record Ideas

Efficient Tarot Card Reader

9839093003

myrichindia@gmail.com

drjagadeeshpillai@facebook

drjagadeeshpillai@instagram

jagadeeshpillai@youtube

www. JAGADEESHPILLAI.com

|| LOKAHA SAMASTHAHA SUKHINO BHAVANTU ||

• 63 •

www.ingramcontent.com/pod-product-compliance
Lightning Source LLC
Chambersburg PA
CBHW070552160726
48003CB00005B/2010